GET THE ANSWERS! History

Q&A ABOUT WESTWARD EXPANSION

By Kathleen Connors

INVESTIGATE!

Enslow PUBLISHING

Please visit our website, www.enslow.com.
For a free color catalog of all our high-quality books, call toll free 1-800-398-2504 or fax 1-877-980-4454.

Library of Congress Cataloging-in-Publication Data
Names: Connors, Kathleen, author.
Title: Q & a about westward expansion / Kathleen Connors.
Other titles: Questions and answers about westward expansion
Description: Buffalo, New York : Enslow Publishing, [2025] | Series: Get the answers! history | Includes index.
Identifiers: LCCN 2024006615 | ISBN 9781978540040 (library binding) | ISBN 9781978540033 (paperback) | ISBN 9781978540057 (ebook)
Subjects: LCSH: United States–Territorial expansion–Juvenile literature–Miscellanea. | West (U.S.)–History–19th century–Juvenile literature–Miscellanea. | Frontier and pioneer life–West (U.S.)–History–19th century–Juvenile literature–Miscellanea.
Classification: LCC E179.5 .C6588 2025 | DDC 978.02–dc23/eng/20240215
LC record available at https://lccn.loc.gov/2024006615

Published in 2025 by
Enslow Publishing
2544 Clinton Street
Buffalo, NY 14224

Portions of this work were originally authored by Lynn George and published as *What Do You Know About Westward Expansion?* All new material in this edition is authored by Kathleen Connors.

Designer: Andrea Davison-Bartolotta
Editor: Kristen Nelson

Photo credits: Cover, p. 1 Keith Lance/iStockphoto.com; series art (question mark backgrounds) Darcraft/Shutterstock.com; p. 4 Everett Collection/Shutterstock.com; p. 5 blinkblink/Shutterstock.com; p. 6 Internet Archive Book Images/Flickr; p. 7 Jose Gil/Shutterstock.com; p. 8 File:Lewis and clark-expedition.jpg/Wikimedia Commons; p. 9 EWY Media/Shutterstock.com; pp. 10, 15, 18, 23 (main), 24 courtesy of Library of Congress; p. 11 frees/Shutterstock.com; p. 12 Leena Robinson/Shutterstock.com; p. 13 Ralf Broskvar/Shutterstock.com; p. 14 catwalker/Shutterstock.com; p. 16 File:Alfred Jacob Miller - Breaking up Camp at Sunrise - Walters 371940142.jpg/Wikimedia Commons; p. 17 File:ColumbiaAmericasGreatHighway040.png/Wikimedia Commons; p. 19 Toledo Lucas County Public Library Digital Collections; p. 20 Campwillowlake/iStockphoto.com; p. 21 File:Trails of Tears en.png/Wikimedia Commons; pp. 22, 23 (inset) Yale University Library/Digital Collections/Beinecke Rare Book and Manuscript Library; p. 26 xavitorrents/Shutterstock.com; p. 27 File:Queen Liliuokalani color.jpg/Wikimedia Commons; p. 28 Chad Robertson Media/Shutterstock.com; p. 29 (inset) Serban Bogdan/Shutterstock.com; p. 29 (main) Porcupen/Shutterstock.com.

Printed in the United States of America

Some of the images in this book illustrate individuals who are models. The depictions do not imply actual situations or events.

CPSIA compliance information: Batch #CS25ENS: For further information contact Enslow Publishing, at 1-800-398-2504.

CONTENTS

Words in the glossary appear in **bold** type the first time they are used in the text.

READY TO GROW

In the Treaty of Paris, signed in 1783, Great Britain officially recognized the United States's independence. It also set the western border of the new nation at the Mississippi River. When this occurred, there were 13 states in the United States. These were the 13 former British colonies.

By 1803, there were 17 states. Vermont, Kentucky, Tennessee, and Ohio had been added. But, the people of the new United States wanted to expand, or grow, even further!

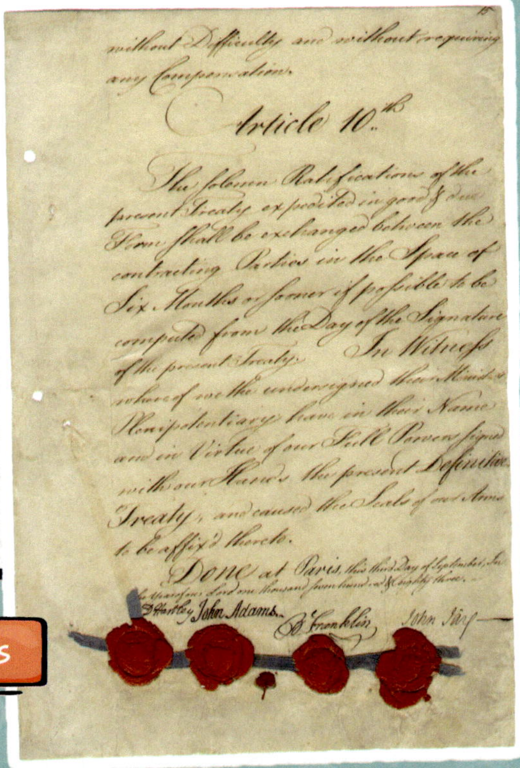
without Difficulty and without requiring any Compensation.

Article 10th.

The solemn Ratification of the present Treaty expedited in good & due Form shall be exchanged between the contracting Parties in the Space of Six Months or sooner if possible to be computed from the Day of the Signature of the present Treaty. In Witness whereof we the undersigned their Ministers Plenipotentiary have in their Name and in Virtue of our Full Powers signed with our Hands the present Definitive Treaty, and caused the Seals of our Arms to be affix'd thereto.

Done at Paris, this third Day of September, In the Year of our Lord one thousand seven hundred & Eighty three.

D Hartley John Adams. B Franklin John Jay

Treaty of Paris

This map shows the 17 states that made up the United States in 1803.

THE BIG ADDITION

QUESTION 1

Whose land is it?

ANSWER

Europeans settled colonies on land that first belonged to Native Americans. Most people living west of the Mississippi River in 1803 were part of these Native groups. As the United States grew, Native people lost their land.

At first, Native Americans lived peacefully with the settlers. However, they fought back when settlers kept taking their land.

QUESTION 2

What happened in 1803?

ANSWER

The U.S. government bought Louisiana from France. Today, this is called the Louisiana Purchase. The United States became twice as big! Louisiana went from the Mississippi River to the Rocky Mountains and from the Gulf of Mexico to Canada.

The Louisiana Purchase cost $15 million—that's only about 4 cents per acre (4,047 sq m).

QUESTION 3

Who explored the Louisiana Purchase?

ANSWER

Meriwether Lewis and William Clark led an expedition, or journey, into the new land. Their group was called the Corps of Discovery. They left from Saint Louis, Missouri, in May 1804.

A Shoshone woman named Sacagawea helped guide the Corps. She acted as an **interpreter** and showed them which plants were good to eat or treat sickness.

QUESTION 4

What did the Corps find out?

ANSWER

President Thomas Jefferson hoped the Corps would find a water route, or path, from the Mississippi River to the Pacific Ocean. They didn't find it—but they did meet Native American groups and map the Upper Mississippi River and its **tributaries**.

By the time the Corps finished their expedition in September 1806, they had documented, or recorded, many plants and animals Americans hadn't known about before!

FROM SEA TO SHINING SEA

QUESTION 5

What is Manifest Destiny?

ANSWER

It is the idea that the United States was **destined** to grow west to the Pacific Ocean—and perhaps beyond it! A newspaper writer first used the term in 1845.

Believers in Manifest Destiny said it was Americans' duty to expand the country. When James K. Polk ran for president at this time, part of his message included favoring expansion.

QUESTION 6

Did Great Britain and the United States really share Oregon?

ANSWER

In 1818, the United States and Great Britain agreed to share land in the Pacific Northwest. In 1846, a border splitting the land was agreed to. The U.S. **territory** would become the states of Washington, Oregon, and Idaho.

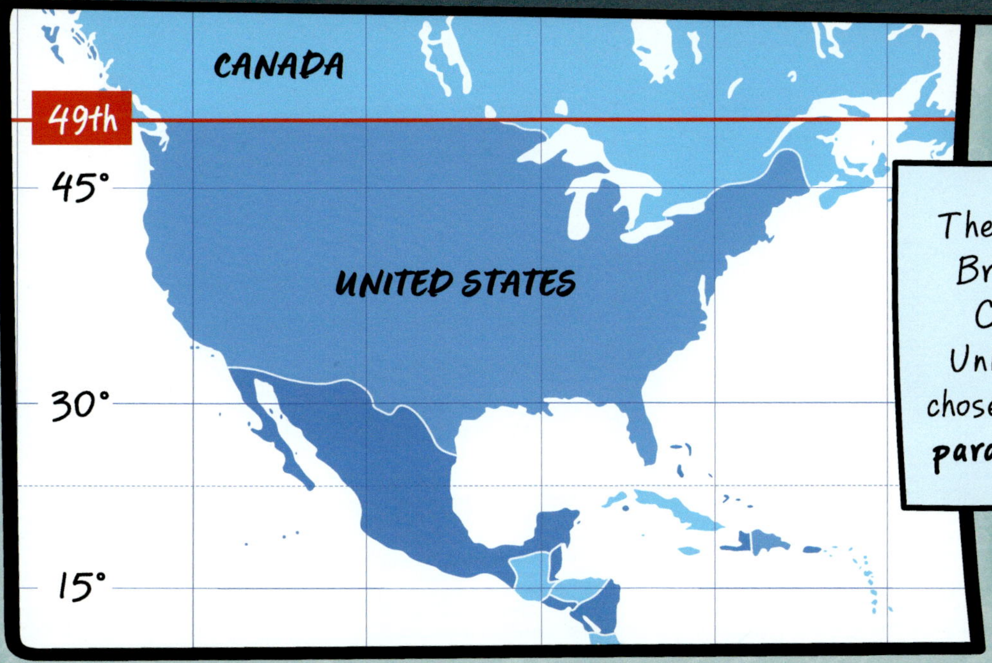

The border between British-controlled Canada and the United States was chosen to be the 49th **parallel**, shown here.

TEXAS AND CALIFORNIA

QUESTION 7

Was Texas part of Mexico first?

ANSWER

Yes, and many people from the United States had settled there. By 1836, they were no longer happy with Mexican rule. Texas declared, or announced, itself a free country! However, Mexican leaders still considered it part of Mexico.

This was one of the flags used by the Texas Republic. It's the same as the Texas state flag today.

Timeline of the Mexican Cession

1835 People in Texas start fighting against Mexican rule.

1836 Texas declares its independence. It tries to become a U.S. state for the first time.

1845 Texas becomes the 28th U.S. state.

1846 The Mexican-American War begins.

1848 The United States wins the war.

Mexico gave up claims to the present-day states of New Mexico, California, Nevada, Utah, most of Arizona, and parts of Colorado, Kansas, Oklahoma, and Wyoming to the United States after the Mexican-American War. Mexico also gave up all claims to Texas. This land is called the Mexican Cession.

QUESTION 8

How many people did the gold rush bring to California?

ANSWER

When gold was discovered in California in January 1848, there were less than 15,000 settlers in California, as well as 150,000 Native peoples. By the following year, there were 100,000 non-Native people!

The prospectors, or gold seekers, that came to California in 1849 were called forty-niners in honor of the year.

QUESTION 9

Did the gold rush help make California a state?

ANSWER

It played a big part. After the United States won the Mexican-American War, those in California thought the U.S. government would take control. When it didn't do so quickly and the population grew, state **representatives** wrote a state **constitution** anyway!

San Francisco harbor, 1851

California became a state on September 9, 1850.

TO THE FRONTIER!

QUESTION 10

How long did a journey on the Oregon Trail take?

ANSWER

It took five to six months. The trail, which was about 2,000 miles (3,200 km) long, began in Independence, Missouri, and ended in Oregon City, Oregon. The Santa Fe Trail was another route many people traveled.

As many as 500,000 people used the Oregon Trail to travel west. Most traveled in wagon trains like this one.

QUESTION 11

What was life on a wagon train like?

ANSWER

Every day was much the same on the trip west. People woke before sunrise. They ate and then started on the trail. They stopped for lunch. They stopped again in the evening. They had dinner and went to bed.

The way west was hard. Many people died along the way of illness and accidents.

QUESTION 12

Did the United States offer free land?

ANSWER

Congress passed the Homestead Act in 1862. It gave 160 acres (65 ha) of land, or homesteads, to anyone who lived on the land and farmed it for five years. Then, they only paid a low **registration** fee.

People who traveled west to start a new life were called homesteaders or pioneers. The land they went to was called the frontier, which means an area of land that has yet to be settled.

QUESTION 13

How hard was pioneer life?

ANSWER

Setting up a homestead wasn't easy. Pioneers had to build a house and farm, as well as take care of and feed their families in the meantime. Many people barely got by.

At first, many homesteaders had to build homes out of sod, or blocks of soil and grass. If they were able, they later built homes from wood, like this log cabin.

NATIVE REMOVAL

QUESTION 14

Where were the Native Americans?

ANSWER

As settlers moved west, they often pushed Native groups out. In addition, throughout the 1800s, the U.S. government passed laws about moving Native Americans to support, or help, the country's expansion.

Belief in Manifest Destiny included the idea that the destiny of expansion was for white Americans only. It was part of why Native groups were removed from their homes.

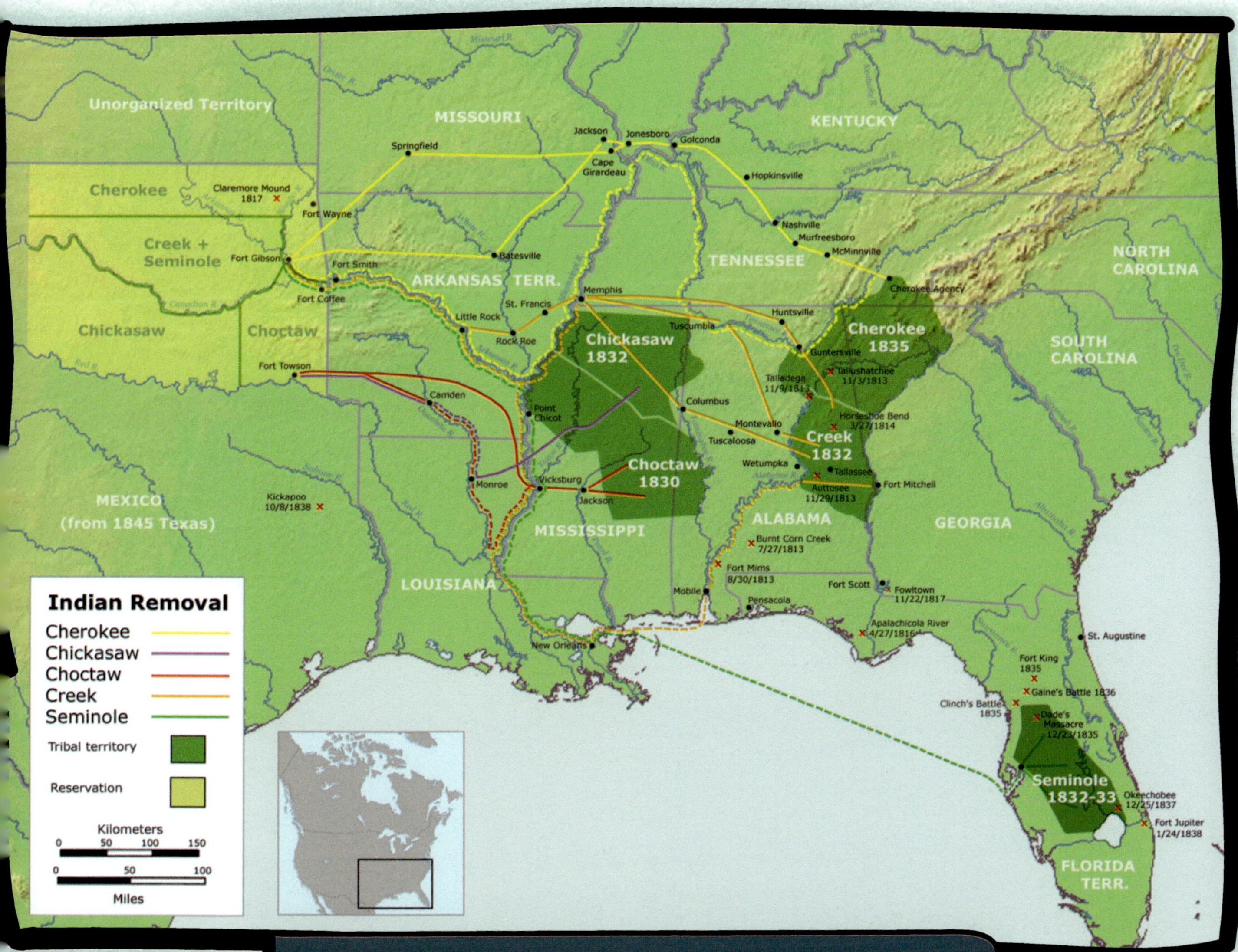

In 1830, the Indian Removal Act started a huge movement of Native people to the western United States. Another law passed in 1851 that moved them again, this time to **reservations** to allow more Americans to go west, among other reasons.

WORKING ON THE RAILROAD

QUESTION 15

Were wagons always the only way west?

ANSWER

People needed a faster way to move themselves and goods across the country. The government decided to build a railroad connecting railways in the East to the West. Work on this transcontinental railroad began in 1863.

Two companies worked to build the railroad: the Central Pacific Railroad and the Union Pacific Railroad. The two lines met in Promontory, Utah, when the line was finished in 1869.

QUESTION 16

How did travel change?

ANSWER

Before the transcontinental railroad, it took months to travel from the Missouri River to California. By rail, it now took around five days! That means goods could move more easily from coast to coast too.

Promontory, Utah

This map shows the length of the transcontinental railroad added between 1863 and 1869.

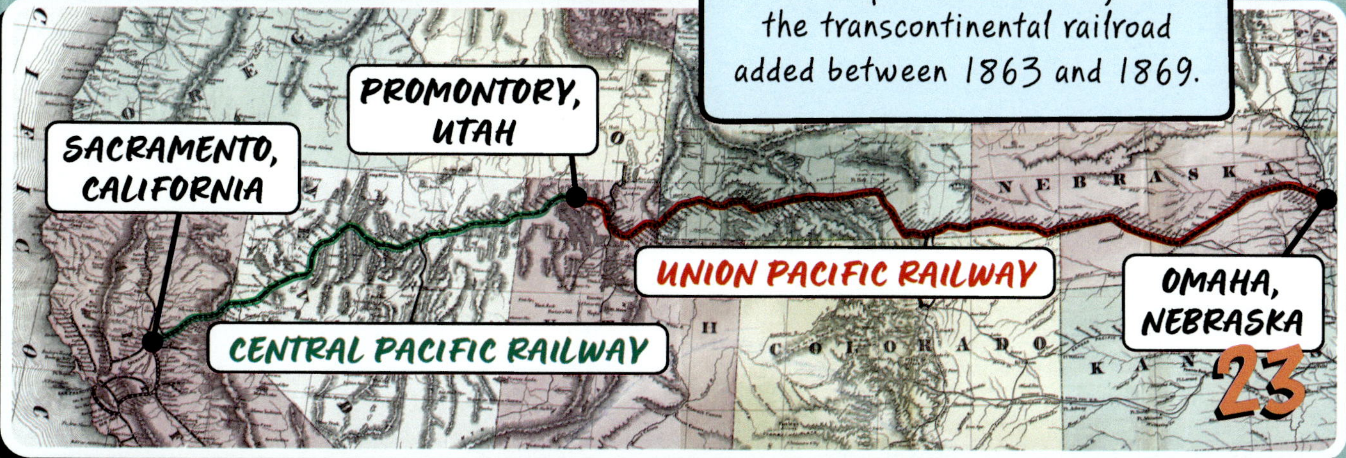

ADDING MORE STATES

QUESTION 17

How is a state added to the United States?

ANSWER

The U.S. Constitution states Congress admits, or brings in, states. Often, areas become territories first. Congress may list conditions to be met before a territory can become a state. Then, the territory sends a state constitution to Congress. Finally, Congress may pass a law to add the state!

Colorado, 1876

States Added Between 1850 and 1890

state	date added to the United States
California	September 9, 1850
Minnesota	May 11, 1858
Oregon	February 14, 1859
Kansas	January 29, 1861
West Virginia	June 20, 1863
Nevada	October 31, 1864
Nebraska	March 1, 1867
Colorado	August 1, 1876
North Dakota	November 2, 1889
South Dakota	November 2, 1889
Montana	November 8, 1889
Washington	November 11, 1889
Idaho	July 3, 1890
Wyoming	July 10, 1890

In 1890, the government said westward expansion was over. The United States had 44 total states then.

QUESTION 18

How long did the United States own Alaska before it became a state?

ANSWER

It was more than 90 years! Russia wanted to sell Alaska to the United States as early as 1859. The **Civil War** stopped the sale. But, the United States bought the territory on October 18, 1867.

Alaska became a state on January 3, 1959.

QUESTION 19

What happened to Hawaii's queen?

ANSWER

When Queen Liliuokalani became queen, the ruler's power had already been greatly reduced. She tried to gain it back but was overthrown by white businessmen and planters in 1893. By 1900, Hawaii was a U.S. territory. It became a state in 1959.

Queen Liliuokalani's family had ruled in Hawaii since 1810. She was only queen for around two years.

QUESTION 20

Will the United States ever expand again?

ANSWER

Even though there is no farther west the United States can grow, one U.S. territory has tried to become a state: Puerto Rico! So far, the people of Puerto Rico have voted to become a state three times, the last in 2020. Congress has yet to admit the territory as a state.

If Puerto Rico is ever added as a state, the government will have to add a 51st star to the U.S. flag!

GLOSSARY

Civil War: A war fought from 1861 to 1865 in the United States between the Union (the Northern states) and the Confederacy (the Southern states).

constitution: The basic laws by which a country or state is governed.

destined: Decided beforehand.

gold rush: The rush to newly found goldfields in search of riches.

interpreter: Someone who helps people who speak different languages talk to each other.

parallel: A line of latitude, or one of the imaginary circles around the surface of Earth running parallel to the equator.

registration: The act of making something part of the official record.

representative: A member of a lawmaking body who acts for voters.

reservation: Area of land set aside by the government for Native Americans to live on.

territory: Part of the United States that is not a state.

tributary: A river that joins a larger river or a lake.

FOR MORE INFORMATION

BOOKS

Quick, Megan. *How Did Pioneer Kids Live?*. Buffalo, NY: Gareth Stevens Publishing, 2024.

Yomtov, Nel. *The Louisiana Purchase: Asking Tough Questions.* North Mankato, MN: Capstone Press, 2021.

WEBSITES

California Gold Rush Facts and History
https://historyforkids.org/california-gold-rush/
Read more about the California gold rush here.

U.S. States and Territories
https://kids.nationalgeographic.com/geography/states
Check out pictures of all the present-day U.S. states and territories.

Westward Expansion
https://education.nationalgeographic.org/resource/resource-library-westward-expansion/
Find maps and read articles about the westward expansion of the United States.

INDEX